BAKING
FOR
SPECIAL OCCASIONS

PUBLICATIONS INTERNATIONAL, LTD.

Favorite All Time Recipes is a trademark of Publications International, Ltd.

Duncan Hines is a registered trademark of Hines-Park Foods, Inc.

Crisco, Crisco Puritan and Butter Flavor Crisco are registered trademarks of The Procter & Gamble Company, Inc.

Project Editor: Cindy Young
Project Art Director: Anita Gindele
Recipe development and testing by The Duncan Hines Kitchens.

This edition published by Publications International, Ltd., 7373 North Cicero Avenue, Lincolnwood, Illinois 60646.

ISBN: 0-7853-0126-7

Pictured on the front cover: Double Berry Layer Cake (*page 26*).

Pictured on the back cover (*top to bottom*): Fudgy Pistachio Cake (*page 64*), Banana Split Cake (*page 78*) and Trifle Spectacular (*page 54*).

First published in the United States.

Manufactured in U.S.A.

8 7 6 5 4 3 2 1

MICROWAVE COOKING
Microwave ovens vary in wattage and power output; cooking times given with microwave directions in this cookbook may need to be adjusted.

BAKING
FOR
SPECIAL OCCASIONS

*B*REAKFAST BUFFET

Peachy Blueberry Crunch

9 Servings

1 package Duncan Hines®
    Bakery Style Blueberry
    Muffin Mix
4 cups peeled, sliced
    peaches (about 4 large)
½ cup water

3 tablespoons brown sugar
½ cup chopped pecans
⅓ cup butter or margarine,
    melted
Whipped topping or ice
    cream (optional)

1. Preheat oven to 350°F.

2. Rinse blueberries from Mix with cold water and drain.

3. Arrange peach slices in ungreased 9-inch square pan. Sprinkle blueberries over peaches. Combine water and brown sugar in liquid measuring cup. Pour over fruit.

4. Combine muffin mix, pecans and melted butter in large bowl. Stir until thoroughly blended. (Mixture will be crumbly.) Sprinkle crumb mixture over fruit. Sprinkle contents of topping packet from Mix over crumb mixture. Bake at 350°F for 50 to 55 minutes or until lightly browned and bubbly. Serve warm with whipped topping, if desired.

> **Tip:** *If peaches are not fully ripened when purchased, place several peaches in a paper bag at room temperature; loosely close and check daily. Peaches are ripe when they give to slight pressure.*

Peachy Blueberry Crunch

Orange Cinnamon Swirl Bread

1 Loaf (12 Slices)

BREAD
- 1 package Duncan Hines® Bakery Style Cinnamon Swirl Muffin Mix
- 1 egg
- ⅔ cup orange juice
- 1 tablespoon grated orange peel

ORANGE GLAZE
- ½ cup confectioners sugar
- 2 to 3 teaspoons orange juice
- 1 teaspoon grated orange peel
- Quartered orange slices, for garnish (optional)

1. Preheat oven to 350°F. Grease and flour 8½×4½×2½-inch loaf pan.

2. **For bread,** combine muffin mix and contents of topping packet from Mix in large bowl. Break up any lumps. Add egg, ⅔ cup orange juice and 1 tablespoon orange peel. Stir until moistened, about 50 strokes. Knead swirl packet from Mix for 10 seconds before opening. Squeeze contents on top of batter. Swirl into batter with knife or spatula, folding from bottom of bowl to get an even swirl. (Do not completely mix into batter.) Pour into pan. Bake at 350°F for 55 to 60 minutes or until toothpick inserted in center comes out clean. Cool in pan 10 minutes. Loosen loaf from pan. Invert onto cooling rack. Turn right-side up. Cool completely.

3. **For orange glaze,** place confectioners sugar in small bowl. Add orange juice, 1 teaspoon at a time, stirring until smooth and desired consistency. Stir in 1 teaspoon orange peel. Drizzle over loaf. Garnish with orange slices, if desired.

Tip: *If glaze becomes too thin, add more confectioners sugar. If glaze is too thick, add more orange juice.*

Orange Cinnamon Swirl Bread

Spring Break Blueberry Coffeecake

9 Servings

TOPPING
- ½ cup flaked coconut
- ¼ cup firmly packed brown sugar
- 2 tablespoons butter or margarine, softened
- 1 tablespoon all-purpose flour

CAKE
- 1 package Duncan Hines® Blueberry Muffin Mix
- 1 can (8 ounces) crushed pineapple with juice, undrained
- 1 egg

1. Preheat oven to 350°F. Grease 9-inch square pan.

2. **For topping,** combine coconut, brown sugar, butter and flour in small bowl. Mix with fork until well blended. Set aside.

3. Rinse blueberries from Mix with cold water and drain.

4. **For cake,** place muffin mix in medium bowl. Break up any lumps. Add pineapple with juice and egg. Stir until moistened, about 50 strokes. Fold in blueberries. Spread in pan. Sprinkle reserved topping over batter. Bake at 350°F for 25 to 30 minutes or until toothpick inserted in center comes out clean. Serve warm or cool completely.

> **Tip:** *To keep blueberries from discoloring batter, drain on paper towels after rinsing.*

Cinnamon Nut Tea Bread   1 Loaf (18 Slices)

1 package Duncan Hines®
    Bakery Style Cinnamon
    Swirl Muffin Mix
¾ cup toasted pecans, finely
    chopped (see Tip)
2 tablespoons all-purpose
    flour

½ teaspoon baking powder
1 egg
⅔ cup water
    Cranberry-Orange Cream
    Cheese (recipe follows)
    Honey Butter (recipe
    follows)

1. Preheat oven to 350°F. Grease and flour 8½×4½×2½-inch loaf pan.

2. Combine muffin mix, contents of topping packet from Mix, chopped pecans, flour and baking powder in medium bowl. Stir until blended. Knead swirl packet from Mix for 10 seconds. Squeeze contents onto dry ingredients. Add egg and water. Stir until thoroughly blended, about 50 strokes. Pour into pan. Bake at 350°F for 65 to 70 minutes or until toothpick inserted in center comes out clean. Cool in pan 10 minutes. Invert onto cooling rack. Turn right-side up. Cool completely.

3. To serve, cut bread into thin slices. Cut each slice in half or cut into fancy shapes, if desired. Spread with Cranberry-Orange Cream Cheese or Honey Butter.

Cranberry-Orange Cream Cheese

1 package (8 ounces) cream
    cheese, softened
1 container (12 ounces)
    cranberry-orange sauce,
    divided

2 to 3 drops red food
    coloring

Combine cream cheese and ¼ cup cranberry-orange sauce in small bowl. Stir with wooden spoon until thoroughly blended. Stir in red food coloring. Spread on bread slices. Garnish with remaining cranberry-orange sauce.

1 cup Spread

Honey Butter

½ cup butter, softened
¼ cup honey

Pecan halves, for garnish

Combine butter and honey in small bowl. Stir with wooden spoon until thoroughly blended. Spread on bread slices. Garnish with pecan halves.

¾ cup Spread

Tip: *To toast pecans, spread in a single layer on baking sheet. Toast in 350°F oven for 5 to 7 minutes or until fragrant. Cool completely.*

Pineapple-Orange Streusel Coffeecake

12 to 16 Servings

STREUSEL

1 package Duncan Hines® Moist Deluxe Pineapple Supreme Cake Mix, divided

2 tablespoons brown sugar

1 teaspoon grated orange peel

½ teaspoon ground cinnamon

⅓ cup coarsely chopped pecans

CAKE

4 eggs

1 package (4-serving size) vanilla instant pudding and pie filling mix

1 cup orange juice

⅓ cup Crisco® Oil or Crisco® Puritan® Oil

GLAZE

1 tablespoon brown sugar

1 tablespoon orange juice

¼ teaspoon vanilla extract

¾ cup confectioners sugar

1 teaspoon grated orange peel

⅓ cup coarsely chopped pecans

1. Preheat oven to 350°F. Grease and flour 10-inch Bundt® pan.

2. **For streusel,** combine 2 tablespoons cake mix, 2 tablespoons brown sugar, 1 teaspoon orange peel and cinnamon in medium bowl. Stir in ⅓ cup pecans. Set aside.

3. **For cake,** combine remaining cake mix, eggs, pudding mix, 1 cup orange juice and oil in large bowl. Beat at medium speed with electric mixer for 2 minutes. Pour into pan. Sprinkle with streusel. Swirl with knife. Bake at 350°F for 50 to 60 minutes or until toothpick inserted in center comes out clean. Cool in pan 25 minutes. Invert onto serving plate.

4. **For glaze,** combine 1 tablespoon brown sugar, 1 tablespoon orange juice and vanilla extract in small bowl. Add confectioners sugar gradually, stirring until smooth. Stir in 1 teaspoon orange peel. Drizzle half the glaze over warm cake. Sprinkle ⅓ cup pecans over glaze. Drizzle remaining glaze over pecans. Serve warm.

> **Tip:** *To reheat leftovers, place serving of coffeecake on microwave-safe plate. Microwave at HIGH (100% power) for 10 to 15 seconds or until warm.*

Cinnamon Rolls

ROLLS
- 1 package Duncan Hines® Moist Deluxe Yellow Cake Mix
- 5 cups all-purpose flour
- 2 packages (¼ ounce each) active dry yeast
- 2½ cups hot water
- Butter or margarine, softened
- Ground cinnamon
- Granulated sugar

TOPPING
- ½ cup butter or margarine, melted
- ¼ cup firmly packed brown sugar
- ¼ cup light corn syrup
- 1 cup chopped nuts

1. Grease two 13×9×2-inch pans.

2. **For rolls,** combine cake mix, flour and yeast in large bowl. Stir until well blended. Stir in hot water. Cover and let rise in warm place for 1 hour or until doubled.

3. Divide dough in half. Roll half the dough into large rectangle on floured surface. Spread with generous amount of softened butter. Sprinkle with cinnamon and granulated sugar. Roll up jelly-roll fashion and cut into 12 slices. Place rolls in one pan. Repeat with remaining dough. Cover and let rise in pans for 30 to 40 minutes or until doubled.

4. Preheat oven to 375°F.

5. **For topping,** combine melted butter, brown sugar, corn syrup and nuts in liquid measuring cup. Pour evenly over rolls. Bake at 375°F for 25 minutes or until light golden brown. Serve warm or cool completely.

> **Tip:** *For a special touch, place 1 cup confectioners sugar in small bowl. Add 1 to 2 tablespoons water, stirring until smooth and desired consistency. Drizzle glaze over baked rolls.*

❧

Yeasty Blueberry Pineapple Coffeecake

8 Servings

COFFEECAKE

1 package Duncan Hines® Blueberry Muffin Mix

1 can (8 ounces) pineapple slices with juice, undrained

1 package (¼ ounce) active dry yeast

1 egg

TOPPING

⅓ cup firmly packed brown sugar

¼ cup butter or margarine, melted

4 maraschino cherries, halved

1. Preheat oven to 350°F.

2. Rinse blueberries from Mix with cold water and drain. Drain pineapple, reserving juice. Halve pineapple slices; set aside.

3. **For coffeecake,** add water to reserved pineapple juice to equal ½ cup. Combine muffin mix and yeast in medium bowl. Break up any lumps. Add egg and ½ cup pineapple liquid. Stir until moistened, about 50 strokes. Set aside.

4. **For topping,** combine brown sugar and melted butter in ungreased 8-inch round cake pan. Spread evenly in bottom of pan. Arrange reserved pineapple in circle. Place cherry halves between pineapple slices. Drop two-thirds of reserved batter by spoonfuls onto topping mixture. Sprinkle with blueberries. Drop remaining batter by spoonfuls onto blueberries. Bake at 350°F for 45 to 50 minutes or until toothpick inserted *halfway* into cake comes out clean. Invert onto serving plate. Serve warm or cool completely.

> **Tip:** *For best flavor, rewarm individual slices on microwave-safe plate. Microwave at HIGH (100% power) for 10 to 15 seconds.*

Yeasty Blueberry Pineapple Coffeecake

PACKED *Lunch* GOODIES

Triple Treat Cookies

3 Dozen Cookies

2 packages Duncan Hines®
  Golden Sugar
  Cookie Mix
2 eggs
2 tablespoons water

¾ cup semi-sweet mini
  chocolate chips
½ cup chopped pecans
½ cup flaked coconut

1. Preheat oven to 375°F.

2. Combine cookie mixes, contents of buttery flavor packets from Mixes, eggs and water in large bowl. Stir until thoroughly blended.

3. Place chocolate chips, pecans and coconut on 3 individual plates. Shape 3 measuring teaspoonfuls dough into 3 balls. Roll 1 ball in chocolate chips, 1 ball in pecans and 1 ball in coconut. Place balls together with sides touching on ungreased baking sheets. Repeat with remaining dough, placing cookies 2 inches apart. Bake at 375°F for 8 to 10 minutes or until light golden brown. Cool 1 minute on baking sheets. Carefully remove to cooling racks. Cool completely. Store in airtight container.

> **Tip:** *To save time when forming dough into balls, use a 1-inch spring-operated cookie scoop. Spring-operated cookie scoops are available at kitchen specialty shops.*

Triple Treat Cookies

Cindy's Fudgy Brownies

24 Brownies

1 package Duncan Hines®
    Fudge Brownie Mix,
    Family Size
1 egg
⅓ cup water

⅓ cup Crisco® Oil or
    Crisco® Puritan® Oil
¾ cup semi-sweet chocolate
    chips
½ cup chopped pecans

1. Preheat oven to 350°F. Grease bottom of 13×9×2-inch pan.

2. Combine brownie mix, egg, water and oil in large bowl. Stir with spoon until well blended, about 50 strokes. Stir in chocolate chips. Spread in pan. Sprinkle with pecans. Bake at 350°F for 25 to 28 minutes or until set. Cool completely. Cut into bars.

> **Tip:** *Overbaking brownies will cause them to become dry. Follow the recommended baking times given in recipes closely.*

Irresistible Lemon Bars

24 Bars

1 package Duncan Hines®
    Golden Sugar Cookie Mix
1½ cups granulated sugar
3 tablespoons all-purpose
    flour
¾ teaspoon baking powder

¼ teaspoon salt
3 eggs, slightly beaten
3 tablespoons lemon juice
1 tablespoon grated lemon
    peel
Confectioners sugar

1. Preheat oven to 350°F.

2. Combine cookie mix and contents of buttery flavor packet from Mix in large bowl. Stir with fork until thoroughly blended. Press evenly into ungreased 13×9×2-inch pan. Bake at 350°F for 14 to 16 minutes or until lightly browned.

3. Combine granulated sugar, flour, baking powder and salt in large bowl. Add eggs, lemon juice and lemon peel. Stir until thoroughly blended. Pour over hot cookie crust. Bake at 350°F for 16 to 18 minutes longer or until lightly browned. Cool completely. Dust with confectioners sugar. Refrigerate until ready to serve. Cut into bars.

> **Tip:** *For an 8- or 9-inch square pan, bake cookie crust at 350°F for 18 to 20 minutes. Pour topping over hot crust. Bake at 350°F for 20 to 22 minutes longer or until lightly browned.*

Cindy's Fudgy Brownies

Orange Pecan Gems

4½ to 5 Dozen Cookies

1 package Duncan Hines®
    Moist Deluxe Orange
    Supreme Cake Mix
1 container (8 ounces)
    vanilla lowfat yogurt

1 egg
2 tablespoons butter or
    margarine, softened
1 cup finely chopped pecans
1 cup pecan halves

1. Preheat oven to 350°F. Grease baking sheets.

2. Combine cake mix, yogurt, egg, butter and chopped pecans in large bowl. Beat at low speed with electric mixer until blended. Drop by rounded teaspoonfuls 2 inches apart onto baking sheets. Press pecan half onto center of each cookie. Bake at 350°F for 11 to 13 minutes or until golden brown. Cool 1 minute on baking sheets. Remove to cooling racks. Cool completely. Store in airtight container.

> **Tip:** *To finely chop pecans quickly, use a food processor fitted with a steel blade and pulse until evenly chopped.*

Baked S'mores

9 Squares

1 package Duncan Hines®
    Golden Sugar Cookie Mix
1 egg
1 tablespoon water

3 bars (1.55 ounces each)
    milk chocolate
1 jar (7 ounces)
    marshmallow creme

1. Preheat oven to 350°F. Grease 8-inch square pan.

2. Combine cookie mix, contents of buttery flavor packet from Mix, egg and water in large bowl. Stir until thoroughly blended. Divide cookie dough in half. Press half the dough evenly into bottom of pan.

3. Cut each milk chocolate bar into 12 sections by following division marks on bars. Arrange chocolate sections into 4 rows with 9 sections in each row.

4. Place spoonfuls of marshmallow creme on top of chocolate. Spread to cover chocolate and cookie dough. Drop remaining cookie dough by teaspoonfuls on top of marshmallow creme. Spread slightly with back of spoon. Bake at 350°F for 25 to 30 minutes or until light golden brown. Cool completely. Cut into squares.

> **Tip:** *Serve Baked S'mores warm for a gooey treat or chilled for a chewy treat.*

Yummy Peanut Butter Bars

18 Bars

BARS
- 1 package Duncan Hines® Peanut Butter Cookie Mix
- 1 egg
- 1 tablespoon water
- ⅓ cup chopped peanuts

WHITE GLAZE
- ½ cup confectioners sugar
- 1 to 2 teaspoons water

CHOCOLATE GLAZE
- ¼ cup semi-sweet chocolate chips
- 2 teaspoons Crisco® Shortening

1. Preheat oven to 350°F.

2. **For bars,** combine cookie mix, contents of peanut butter packet from Mix, egg and 1 tablespoon water in large bowl. Stir until thoroughly blended. Stir in peanuts. Spread in ungreased 8-inch square pan. Bake at 350°F for 23 to 25 minutes or until edges are light golden brown. Cool completely.

3. **For white glaze,** place confectioners sugar in small bowl. Add water, 1 teaspoon at a time, stirring until smooth and desired consistency. Drizzle over cooled bars.

4. **For chocolate glaze,** place chocolate chips and shortening in small resealable plastic bag; seal. Place bag in bowl of hot water for several minutes. Dry with paper towel. Knead until blended and chocolate is smooth. Snip pinpoint hole in corner of bag. Drizzle chocolate glaze over white glaze. Allow glazes to set before cutting into bars.

> **Tip:** *For a special presentation, cut cookies into diamond or triangle shapes instead of bars.*

Lemon Poppy Seed Cupcakes   30 Cupcakes

CUPCAKES
- 1 package Duncan Hines® Moist Deluxe Lemon Supreme Cake Mix
- 3 eggs
- 1⅓ cups water
- ⅓ cup Crisco® Oil or Crisco® Puritan® Oil
- 3 tablespoons poppy seed

LEMON FROSTING
- 1 container (16 ounces) Duncan Hines® Creamy Homestyle Vanilla Frosting
- 1 teaspoon grated lemon peel
- ¼ teaspoon lemon extract
- 3 to 4 drops yellow food coloring
- Yellow and orange gumdrops, for garnish

1. Preheat oven to 350°F. Place 30 (2½-inch) paper liners in muffin cups.

2. **For cupcakes,** combine cake mix, eggs, water, oil and poppy seed in large bowl. Beat at medium speed with electric mixer for 2 minutes. Fill paper liners about half full. Bake at 350°F for 18 to 21 minutes or until toothpick inserted in center comes out clean. Cool in pans 5 minutes. Remove to cooling racks. Cool completely.

3. **For lemon frosting,** combine Vanilla frosting, lemon peel and lemon extract in small bowl. Tint with yellow food coloring to desired color. Frost cupcakes with lemon frosting. Decorate with gumdrops.

Tip: *Store poppy seed in an airtight container in the refrigerator or freezer.*

Special Chocolate Chip Sandwiches

18 Sandwich Cookies

1 package Duncan Hines®
   Chocolate Chip
   Cookie Mix
1 egg
2 teaspoons water

8 ounces chocolate-flavored
   candy coating
¼ cup chopped sliced
   natural almonds

1. Preheat oven to 375°F.

2. Combine cookie mix, contents of buttery flavor packet from Mix, egg and water in large bowl. Stir until thoroughly blended. Drop by rounded teaspoonfuls 2 inches apart onto ungreased baking sheets. Bake at 375°F for 8 to 10 minutes or until light golden brown. Cool 1 minute on baking sheets. Remove to cooling racks. Cool completely.

3. Place chocolate candy coating in small saucepan. Melt on low heat, stirring frequently until smooth.

4. To assemble, spread about ½ teaspoon melted coating on bottom of one cookie; top with second cookie. Press together to make sandwiches. Repeat with remaining cookies. Dip one-third of each sandwich cookie in remaining melted coating and sprinkle with chopped almonds. Place on cooling racks until coating is set. Store between layers of waxed paper in airtight container.

> **Tip:** *Place waxed paper under cooling racks to catch chocolate coating drips and to make clean-up easier.*

Special Chocolate Chip Sandwiches

FABULOUS
After Dinner
DESSERTS

Double Berry Layer Cake   12 Servings

1 package Duncan Hines®
    Moist Deluxe Strawberry
    Supreme Cake Mix
²⁄₃ cup strawberry jam,
    divided
2½ cups fresh blueberries,
    rinsed, drained and
    divided

1 container (8 ounces)
    frozen whipped topping,
    thawed and divided
    Fresh strawberry slices, for
    garnish

1. Preheat oven to 350°F. Grease and flour two 9-inch round cake pans.

2. Prepare, bake and cool cake following package directions for basic recipe.

3. Place one cake layer on serving plate. Spread with ⅓ cup strawberry jam. Arrange 1 cup blueberries on jam. Spread half the whipped topping to within ½ inch of cake edge. Place second cake layer on top. Repeat with remaining ⅓ cup strawberry jam, 1 cup blueberries and remaining whipped topping. Garnish with strawberry slices and remaining ½ cup blueberries. Refrigerate until ready to serve.

> **Tip:** *For best results, cut cake with serrated knife;*
> *clean knife after each slice.*

Double Berry Layer Cake

Chocolate Cherry Torte

12 to 16 Servings

1 package Duncan Hines®
    Moist Deluxe Devil's
    Food Cake Mix
1 can (21 ounces) cherry pie
    filling
¼ teaspoon almond extract

1 container (8 ounces)
    frozen whipped topping,
    thawed and divided
¼ cup toasted sliced
    almonds, for garnish
    (see Tip)

1. Preheat oven to 350°F. Grease and flour two 9-inch round cake pans.

2. Prepare, bake and cool cake following package directions for basic recipe. Combine cherry pie filling and almond extract in small bowl. Stir.

3. To assemble, place one cake layer on serving plate. Spread with 1 cup whipped topping, then half the pie filling mixture. Top with second cake layer. Spread remaining pie filling mixture to within 1½ inches of edge. Decorate cake edge with remaining whipped topping, as desired. Garnish with sliced almonds.

> **Tip:** *To toast almonds, spread in a single layer on baking sheet. Bake at 325°F for 4 to 6 minutes or until fragrant and golden.*

Macaroon Brownies

24 Brownies

1 package Duncan Hines®
    Fudge Brownie Mix,
    Family Size
2 egg whites
½ cup sugar

¼ teaspoon almond extract
1 cup finely chopped
    almonds
1 cup flaked coconut

1. Preheat oven to 350°F. Grease bottom of 13×9×2-inch pan.

2. Prepare brownies following package directions for cake-like brownies. Bake at 350°F for 25 minutes or until set. Place egg whites in medium bowl. Beat at high speed with electric mixer until foamy and double in volume. Beat in sugar gradually, beating until meringue forms firm peaks. Add almond extract. Fold in almonds and coconut. Spread over warm brownies. Bake for 12 to 14 minutes longer or until meringue is set and lightly browned. Cool completely. Cut into bars.

> **Tip:** *Spread meringue to edges of pan to prevent shrinking.*

Chocolate Cherry Torte

Triple Orange Delight

12 to 16 Servings

1 package Duncan Hines®
    Angel Food Cake Mix
2 cans (11 ounces each)
    mandarin orange
    segments, undrained
2 packages (4-serving size
    each) orange flavored
    gelatin

1 quart orange sherbet
1 container (12 ounces)
    frozen whipped topping,
    thawed
Additional whipped
    topping, for garnish
Mint leaves, for garnish

1. Preheat oven to 375°F.

2. Prepare, bake and cool cake following package directions.

3. Drain mandarin oranges, reserving juice. Set mandarin oranges aside. Bring 1 cup reserved juice to boil. Stir in gelatin until dissolved. Pour into large bowl. Add sherbet, stirring until melted. Fold in whipped topping.

4. To assemble, brush loose crust from cake with paper towel. Trim bottom crust from cake. Tear cake into bite-size pieces. Place half the cake pieces in ungreased 13×9×2-inch pan. Reserve 12 to 16 mandarin oranges in refrigerator for garnish. Cut remaining mandarin oranges into pieces. Place half the orange pieces over cake pieces. Cover with half the sherbet mixture. Repeat with remaining cake pieces, orange pieces and sherbet mixture. Refrigerate overnight.

5. To serve, cut dessert into squares. Garnish servings with reserved mandarin oranges, dollops of additional whipped topping and mint leaves.

> **Tip:** *Drain orange segments on paper towels to
> absorb excess moisture.*

Fancy Walnut Brownies

24 Brownies

BROWNIES

1 package Duncan Hines®
    Chocolate Lovers'
    Walnut Brownie Mix

1 egg

⅓ cup water
⅓ cup Crisco® Oil or
    Crisco® Puritan® Oil

GLAZE

4½ cups confectioners sugar
½ cup milk or water

24 walnut halves, for garnish

CHOCOLATE DRIZZLE

⅓ cup semi-sweet chocolate
    chips

1 tablespoon Crisco®
    Shortening

1. Preheat oven to 350°F. Place 24 (2-inch) foil liners on baking sheets.

2. **For brownies,** combine brownie mix, egg, water and oil in large bowl. Stir with spoon until well blended, about 50 strokes. Stir in contents of walnut packet from Mix. Fill foil liners with 2 generous tablespoons batter. Bake at 350°F for 20 to 25 minutes or until set. Cool completely. Remove liners. Turn brownies upside down on cooling rack.

3. **For glaze,** combine confectioners sugar and milk in medium bowl. Blend until smooth. Spoon glaze over first brownie to completely cover. Top immediately with walnut half. Repeat with remaining brownies. Allow glaze to set.

4. **For chocolate drizzle,** place chocolate chips and shortening in resealable plastic bag; seal. Place bag in bowl of hot water for several minutes. Dry with paper towel. Knead until blended and chocolate is smooth. Snip pinpoint hole in corner of bag. Drizzle chocolate over brownies. Store in single layer in airtight containers.

> **Tip:** *Place waxed paper under cooling rack to catch excess glaze.*

Beautiful Strawberry Cake   12 to 16 Servings

2 bars (2 ounces each) white
    chocolate baking bars

CAKE
1 package Duncan Hines®
    Moist Deluxe Strawberry
    Supreme Cake Mix
3 eggs

1⅓ cups water
⅓ cup Crisco® Oil or
    Crisco® Puritan® Oil

FILLING and FROSTING
½ cup seedless red raspberry
    preserves (see Tip)
1 container (16 ounces)
    Duncan Hines® Creamy
    Homestyle Vanilla
    Frosting

Fresh raspberries, for
    garnish
Confectioners sugar, for
    garnish

1. For white chocolate shavings, warm 1 white chocolate baking bar
(2 ounces) in microwave oven at HIGH (100% power) for 5 to
10 seconds. Pull vegetable peeler firmly across flat side of bar to make
large shavings. Continue until shavings can no longer be made. Reserve
scrap pieces of white chocolate. Repeat for second white chocolate
baking bar. Set shavings aside. Grate or finely chop reserved scrap pieces
of white chocolate to equal ½ cup. Set grated white chocolate aside.

2. Preheat oven to 350°F. Grease and flour two 8- or 9-inch square pans.

3. **For cake,** combine cake mix, eggs, water and oil in large bowl. Beat at
medium speed with electric mixer for 2 minutes. Stir in reserved grated
white chocolate. Pour into pans. Bake at 350°F for 33 to 36 minutes for
8-inch pans (28 to 31 minutes for 9-inch pans) or until toothpick
inserted in center comes out clean. Cool in pans 15 minutes. Invert onto
cooling racks. Cool completely.

4. **For filling and frosting,** place one cake layer on serving plate. Spread
with red raspberry preserves. Top with second cake layer. Frost sides and
top with Vanilla frosting. Arrange reserved shavings on top of cake.
Garnish with fresh raspberries. Dust with confectioners sugar just before
serving.

Tip: *If seedless red raspberry preserves are unavailable, you can
remove the seeds easily. Strain warmed preserves through a fine
sieve into a small bowl.*

Fruit 'n' Spice Parfaits

6 to 8 Servings

1 package Duncan Hines®
    Moist Deluxe Spice
    Cake Mix
1 can (14 ounces)
    sweetened condensed
    milk
1 cup cold water
1 package (4-serving size)
    vanilla instant pudding
    and pie filling mix

2 cups whipping cream,
    chilled
2 tablespoons apple brandy
    or apple juice
4½ cups fresh mixed summer
    fruit, divided
1½ cups frozen whipped
    topping, thawed

1. Preheat oven to 350°F. Grease and flour two 9-inch round cake pans (see Tip).

2. Prepare, bake and cool cake following package directions for basic recipe. Cut one cake layer into 1-inch cubes. Freeze other cake layer for later use.

3. Combine sweetened condensed milk and water in large bowl. Stir until blended. Add pudding mix. Beat until thoroughly blended. Refrigerate 5 minutes. Place 2 cups whipping cream in large bowl. Beat at high speed with electric mixer until stiff peaks form. Fold into cooled pudding mixture.

4. To assemble, sprinkle cake cubes with apple brandy. Slice fruit, if necessary. Layer one-third of pudding mixture, half the cake cubes and 2 cups fresh fruit in parfait dishes. Repeat layers. Top with remaining one-third pudding mixture. Garnish with whipped topping and remaining ½ cup fresh fruit. Refrigerate until ready to serve.

Tip: *Instead of baking the second cake layer, prepare*
12 cupcakes for the kids.

Chiffon Cake with Citrus Sauce and Fresh Fruit

12 to 16 Servings

CAKE

1 package Duncan Hines® Angel Food Cake Mix
1 cup water
¾ cup Crisco® Oil or Crisco® Puritan® Oil

3 eggs
¼ cup all-purpose flour
2 tablespoons grated lemon peel
½ teaspoon vanilla extract

CITRUS SAUCE

1 cup sugar
⅓ cup orange juice
1 egg, lightly beaten
1 tablespoon lemon juice
1 teaspoon grated lemon peel
1 cup whipping cream, whipped

Fresh strawberries, sliced, for garnish
Fresh blueberries, for garnish
Kiwifruit, peeled and sliced, for garnish

1. Preheat oven to 350°F.

2. **For cake,** combine Egg White Packet (blue "A" packet) from Mix and water in large bowl. Beat at low speed with electric mixer for 1 minute. Beat at high speed until very stiff peaks form; set aside. Combine Cake Flour Mixture (red "B" packet) from Mix, oil, 3 eggs, flour, 2 tablespoons lemon peel and vanilla extract in large bowl. Beat at low speed with electric mixer until blended. Beat at medium speed for 3 minutes. Fold beaten egg white mixture into lemon batter. Pour batter into ungreased 10-inch tube pan. Run knife through batter to remove air bubbles. Bake at 350°F for 40 to 45 minutes or until toothpick inserted in center comes out clean. Cool following package directions.

3. **For citrus sauce,** combine sugar, orange juice, 1 egg, lemon juice and 1 teaspoon lemon peel in heavy 1-quart saucepan. Cook on medium heat for 10 minutes, stirring constantly, until mixture just comes to a boil. Remove from heat. Refrigerate until chilled. Fold in whipped cream.

4. To serve, cut cake into individual servings. Spoon sauce over cake slices. Garnish with strawberry slices, blueberries and kiwifruit slices.

Tip: *To obtain the most juice from lemons, bring them to room temperature, then roll them on the countertop before squeezing.*

Chiffon Cake with Citrus Sauce and Fresh Fruit

Chocolate Streusel Cake

12 to 16 Servings

STREUSEL

1 package Duncan Hines®
   Moist Deluxe Devil's
   Food Cake Mix, divided
1 cup finely chopped pecans

2 tablespoons brown sugar
2 teaspoons ground
   cinnamon

CAKE

3 eggs
1⅓ cups water

½ cup Crisco® Oil or
   Crisco® Puritan® Oil

TOPPING

1 container (8 ounces)
   frozen whipped topping,
   thawed
3 tablespoons sifted
   unsweetened cocoa

Chopped pecans, for
   garnish (optional)
Chocolate curls, for
   garnish (optional)

1. Preheat oven to 350°F. Grease and flour 10-inch Bundt® pan.

2. **For streusel,** combine 2 tablespoons cake mix, 1 cup pecans, brown sugar and cinnamon. Set aside.

3. **For cake,** combine remaining cake mix, eggs, water and oil in large bowl. Beat at medium speed with electric mixer for 2 minutes. Pour two-thirds of batter into pan. Sprinkle with reserved streusel. Pour remaining batter evenly over streusel. Bake at 350°F for 55 to 60 minutes or until toothpick inserted in center comes out clean. Cool in pan 25 minutes. Invert onto serving plate. Cool completely.

4. **For topping,** place whipped topping in medium bowl. Fold in cocoa until blended. Spread on cooled cake. Garnish with chopped pecans and chocolate curls, if desired. Refrigerate until ready to serve.

> **Tip:** *For chocolate curls, warm chocolate in microwave oven at HIGH (100% power) for 5 to 10 seconds. Make chocolate curls by holding a sharp vegetable peeler against flat side of chocolate block and bringing blade towards you. Apply firm pressure for thicker, more open curls or light pressure for tighter curls.*

Chocolate Streusel Cake

Raspberry Sherbet
Brownie Dessert

12 to 16 Servings

1 package Duncan Hines®
    Chocolate Lovers'
    Double Fudge
    Brownie Mix
2 eggs
⅓ cup water
¼ cup Crisco® Oil or
    Crisco® Puritan® Oil
½ gallon raspberry sherbet,
    softened

1 package (12 ounces)
    frozen dry pack red
    raspberries, thawed and
    undrained
⅓ cup sugar
    Fresh raspberries, for
    garnish

1. Preheat oven to 350°F. Grease bottom of 13×9×2-inch pan.

2. Combine brownie mix, contents of fudge packet from Mix, eggs, water and oil in large bowl. Stir with spoon until well blended, about 50 strokes. Spread in pan. Bake and cool brownies following package directions. Spread softened sherbet over cooled brownies. Cover and freeze for 3 to 4 hours or overnight until firm.

3. For raspberry sauce, combine thawed raspberries with juice and sugar in small saucepan. Bring to a boil. Simmer until berries are soft. Push mixture through sieve into small bowl to remove seeds. Cool completely.

4. To serve, cut dessert into squares. Spoon raspberry sauce over each serving. Garnish with fresh raspberries.

Tip: *Raspberries are most plentiful during June and July. They should be plump with a hollow core. Plan to use them within 1 or 2 days after purchase.*

NO-CHOLESTEROL
Anytime
TREATS

❧

Cinnamon Ripple Cake   12 to 16 Servings

1 package Duncan Hines® Angel Food Cake Mix
1 tablespoon *plus* ¼ teaspoon ground cinnamon, divided

1½ cups frozen lite whipped topping, thawed

1. Preheat oven to 375°F.

2. Prepare cake following package directions. Spoon one-fourth of batter into ungreased 10-inch tube pan. Spread evenly. Sprinkle 1 teaspoon cinnamon over batter with small fine sieve. Repeat layering 2 more times. Top with remaining cake batter. Bake and cool following package directions.

3. Combine whipped topping and remaining ¼ teaspoon cinnamon in small bowl. Serve with cake slices.

Tip: *For angel food cakes, always use a totally grease-free cake pan to get the best volume.*

Cinnamon Ripple Cake

Glazed Ribbon Dessert

24 Servings

1 package Duncan Hines®
    Moist Deluxe White
    Cake Mix
¾ cup strawberry preserves
6 strawberries, halved

1 to 2 peaches, thinly sliced
1 cup peach preserves
    Mint leaves, for garnish
    (optional)

1. Preheat oven to 350°F. Grease and flour 13×9×2-inch pan.

2. Prepare, bake and cool cake following package directions for No Cholesterol recipe. Remove from pan.

3. Split cake in half horizontally (see Tip). Place bottom cake layer on serving plate. Spread with strawberry preserves. Place top cake layer on top of strawberry preserves. Score top with knife to make 24 servings. Alternate strawberry halves and peach slices to form desired design. Heat peach preserves; press through sieve. Brush fruit and top of cake with warmed preserves to glaze. Garnish with mint leaves, if desired.

> **Tip:** *Lift top cake layer with foil-covered, cardboard rectangle.*

Banana Blueberry Muffins

12 Muffins

1 package Duncan Hines®
    Bakery Style Blueberry
    Muffin Mix
2 egg whites

½ cup water
1 medium-size ripe banana,
    mashed (about ½ cup)

1. Preheat oven to 400°F. Place 12 (2½-inch) paper liners in muffin cups.

2. Rinse blueberries from Mix with cold water and drain.

3. Empty muffin mix into bowl. Break up any lumps. Add egg whites, water and mashed banana. Stir until moistened, about 50 strokes. Fold in blueberries. Fill paper liners two-thirds full. Sprinkle with contents of topping packet from Mix. Bake at 400°F for 18 to 22 minutes or until toothpick inserted in center comes out clean. Cool in pan 5 to 10 minutes. Serve warm or cool completely.

> **Tip:** *To reheat leftover muffins, wrap muffins tightly in foil. Place in 400°F oven for 10 to 15 minutes.*

Glazed Ribbon Dessert

Strawberry Bars

16 Bars

1 package Duncan Hines®
    Golden Sugar
    Cookie Mix
1 teaspoon grated lemon
    peel

¼ teaspoon ground
    cinnamon
1 egg white
¾ cup strawberry preserves
    Confectioners sugar

1. Preheat oven to 350°F. Grease sides of 9-inch square pan (see Tip).

2. Combine cookie mix, lemon peel and cinnamon in large bowl. Add contents of buttery flavor packet from Mix and egg white. Stir until thoroughly blended. Press half the dough into bottom of pan. Spread with preserves. Make ropes with remaining dough to form lattice top over preserves (see Photo). Bake at 350°F for 30 to 32 minutes or until golden. Cool completely. Dust with confectioners sugar. Cut into bars.

> **Tip:** *Strawberry Bars will be easier to remove from the pan if the sides have been greased.*

Chocolate Banana Cake

12 to 16 Servings

1 package Duncan Hines®
    Moist Deluxe Swiss
    Chocolate Cake Mix
1½ cups light vanilla nonfat
    yogurt, divided

2 medium bananas, sliced
    and divided
1 tablespoon chopped
    pecans

1. Preheat oven to 350°F. Grease and flour 10-inch tube pan.

2. Prepare, bake and cool cake following package directions for No Cholesterol recipe.

3. Split cake into thirds horizontally. Place bottom cake layer on serving plate. Spread ½ cup yogurt on cake. Arrange half the banana slices on yogurt. Place middle cake layer on top of bananas. Repeat with ½ cup yogurt and remaining banana slices. Place top cake layer on top of bananas. Glaze with remaining ½ cup yogurt. Sprinkle with pecans. Refrigerate until ready to serve.

> **Tip:** *To save time, simply cut cake into serving slices, top with yogurt and garnish with banana slices and chopped pecans.*

Zucchini Muffins

12 Muffins

1 package Duncan Hines®
    Bakery Style Cinnamon
    Swirl Muffin Mix
½ teaspoon baking powder

2 egg whites
⅔ cup water
½ cup grated zucchini

1. Preheat oven to 400°F. Grease 12 (2½-inch) muffin cups (or use paper liners).

2. Combine muffin mix and baking powder in large bowl. Break up any lumps. Add egg whites, water and zucchini. Stir until well blended, about 50 strokes.

3. Knead swirl packet from Mix for 10 seconds before opening. Cut off one end of swirl packet. Squeeze contents on top of batter. Swirl into batter with knife or spatula, folding from bottom of bowl to get an even swirl. (Do not completely mix into batter.) Spoon batter evenly into muffin cups. Sprinkle with contents of topping packet from Mix. Bake at 400°F for 20 to 25 minutes or until toothpick inserted in center comes out clean. Cool in pan 5 to 10 minutes. Serve warm or cool completely.

> **Tip:** *Zucchini can be grated ahead and frozen. Thaw and drain well before using.*

Lemon Raspberry Chocolate Delight

12 to 16 Servings

1 package Duncan Hines® Moist Deluxe Lemon Supreme Cake Mix
3 tablespoons margarine
¼ cup *plus* 2 tablespoons sugar
2 tablespoons unsweetened cocoa
2 tablespoons light corn syrup
¼ cup water
1 teaspoon vanilla extract
2 pints lemon sorbet
1 pint fresh raspberries, for garnish
Mint leaves, for garnish

1. Preheat oven to 350°F. Grease and flour 13×9×2-inch pan.

2. Prepare, bake and cool cake following package directions for No Cholesterol recipe.

3. Melt margarine on low heat in small saucepan. Remove from heat. Add sugar, cocoa, corn syrup and water. Cook on low heat, stirring constantly, until sauce is smooth and begins to boil. Remove from heat. Stir in vanilla extract. Cool slightly.

4. To serve, cut cake into squares. Top each square with scoop of lemon sorbet. Drizzle with 1 tablespoon cocoa sauce. Garnish with fresh raspberries and mint leaves.

> **Tip:** *To save time, purchase chocolate syrup to use in place of cocoa sauce.*

Lemon Raspberry Chocolate Delight

SPECIAL CELEBRATIONS

❧

May Day Cake

12 to 16 Servings

1 package Duncan Hines®
  Moist Deluxe Strawberry
  Supreme Cake Mix
2 containers (16 ounces
  each) Duncan Hines®
  Creamy Homestyle
  Cream Cheese Frosting

Fresh flowers (roses,
pansies or daisies), for
garnish (see Tip)

1. Preheat oven to 350°F. Grease and flour two 8-inch round cake pans.

2. Prepare, bake and cool cake following package directions for basic recipe.

3. Fill and frost cake with Cream Cheese frosting. Garnish with fresh flowers just before serving.

Tip: *Be sure to use only non-toxic flowers. Rinse fresh flowers with cool water and dry with paper towels. Place small piece of plastic wrap under flowers that rest on cake.*

May Day Cake

Trifle Spectacular

10 to 12 Servings

1 package Duncan Hines® Moist Deluxe Devil's Food Cake Mix
1 can (14 ounces) sweetened condensed milk
1 cup cold water
1 package (4-serving size) vanilla instant pudding and pie filling mix
2 cups whipping cream, whipped
2 tablespoons orange juice, divided
2½ cups sliced fresh strawberries, divided
1 pint fresh raspberries, divided
2 kiwifruit, peeled and sliced, divided
1½ cups frozen whipped topping, thawed, for garnish
Mint leaves, for garnish (optional)

1. Preheat oven to 350°F. Grease and flour two 9-inch round cake pans.

2. Prepare, bake and cool cake following package directions for basic recipe. Cut one cake layer into 1-inch cubes. Freeze other cake layer for later use.

3. Combine sweetened condensed milk and water in large bowl. Stir until blended. Add pudding mix. Beat until thoroughly blended. Chill 5 minutes. Fold whipped cream into pudding mixture.

4. To assemble, spread 2 cups pudding mixture into 3-quart trifle dish (or 3-quart clear glass bowl with straight sides). Arrange half the cake cubes over pudding mixture. Sprinkle with 1 tablespoon orange juice. Layer with 1 cup strawberry slices, half the raspberries and one-third of kiwifruit slices. Repeat layers. Top with remaining pudding mixture. Garnish with whipped topping, remaining ½ cup strawberry slices, kiwifruit slices and mint leaves, if desired.

Tip: *Since the different layers contribute to the beauty of this recipe, arrange the fruit pieces to show attractively along the sides of the trifle dish.*

Tropical Ambrosia Cake
12 to 16 Servings

1 package Duncan Hines®
  Moist Deluxe Orange
  Supreme Cake Mix
1 package (8 ounces) cream
  cheese, softened
1 jar (14 ounces)
  marshmallow creme

1 can (8 ounces) pineapple
  tidbits, drained
1 cup seedless grapes,
  halved
3 bananas, sliced
1 cup toasted coconut
  (see Tip)

1. Preheat oven to 350°F. Grease and flour 13×9×2-inch pan.

2. Prepare, bake and cool cake following package directions for basic recipe.

3. Place cream cheese in small bowl. Beat at low speed with electric mixer until smooth. Add marshmallow creme. Beat until blended. Combine pineapple tidbits, grape halves and banana slices in medium bowl. To serve, spoon cream cheese mixture over individual cake pieces. Top with fruit mixture and toasted coconut.

> **Tip:** *To toast coconut, spread evenly on baking sheet. Toast in 350°F oven for 3 minutes. Stir and toast 1 to 2 minutes longer or until light golden brown.*

Strawberry Cookie Tarts
12 Servings

COOKIES
1 package Duncan Hines®
  Moist Deluxe French
  Vanilla Cake Mix

¾ cup Butter Flavor Crisco®
1 egg
2 tablespoons milk

FILLING
1 quart fresh strawberries
¼ cup granulated sugar
1 cup whipping cream,
  chilled

2 tablespoons confectioners
  sugar
Additional confectioners
  sugar, for garnish
Mint leaves, for garnish

1. Preheat oven to 375°F.

2. **For cookies,** combine cake mix, Butter Flavor Crisco®, egg and milk in large bowl. Beat at low speed with electric mixer until blended. Shape dough into 24 (1½-inch) balls. Place balls 2 inches apart on ungreased baking sheets. Bake at 375°F for 10 minutes or until light golden brown around edges. *Do not overbake* (see Tip). Cool 2 minutes on baking sheets. Remove to cooling racks.

3. **For filling,** cut 6 strawberries in half; set aside. Slice remaining strawberries into large bowl. Stir in granulated sugar. Refrigerate. Combine whipping cream and 2 tablespoons confectioners sugar in medium bowl. Beat at high speed until soft peaks form.

4. To assemble each tart, place one cookie on serving plate. Cover with ¼ cup sliced strawberries. Dollop with 2 tablespoons whipped cream mixture. Place second cookie on top. Dust with additional confectioners sugar. Garnish tarts with reserved strawberry halves and mint leaves.

> **Tip:** *These chewy-style cookies are slightly puffed when ready to be removed from oven and will settle during cooling.*

Easter Basket Brownies   18 Easter Baskets

BROWNIES

1 package Duncan Hines® Chocolate Lovers' Milk Chocolate Chunk Brownie Mix

2 eggs
⅓ cup water
⅓ cup Crisco® Oil or Crisco® Puritan® Oil

TOPPING

Green food coloring
½ teaspoon water
1 cup flaked coconut
1 container (16 ounces) Duncan Hines® Creamy Homestyle Chocolate or Vanilla Frosting

Assorted Easter candies
9 (12-inch) chenille stems, cut in half
Narrow pastel ribbon

1. Preheat oven to 350°F. Place 18 (2½-inch) foil liners in muffin cups.

2. **For brownies,** combine brownie mix, eggs, ⅓ cup water and oil in large bowl. Stir with spoon until well blended, about 50 strokes. Fill foil liners two-thirds full. Bake at 350°F for 20 to 24 minutes or until set. Cool completely.

3. **For topping,** combine several drops green food coloring and ½ teaspoon water in small bowl. Add coconut. Toss with fork until evenly tinted. Spread Chocolate frosting on each brownie. Sprinkle with tinted coconut. Top with assorted Easter candies. Insert one chenille stem half in each brownie to create handle. Cut ribbon into bow-sized pieces. Tie bows on sides of handles.

> **Tip:** *Arrange Easter Basket Brownies on a doily-lined platter.*

Keyboard Cake

16 to 20 Servings

1 package Duncan Hines®
    Moist Deluxe Cake Mix
    (any flavor)
1 container (16 ounces)
    Duncan Hines® Creamy
    Homestyle Vanilla
    Frosting, divided

1 container (16 ounces)
    Duncan Hines® Creamy
    Homestyle Chocolate
    Frosting, divided
2 bars (1.55 ounces each)
    milk chocolate
    Vanilla milk chips

1. Preheat oven to 350°F. Grease and flour 13×9×2-inch pan.

2. Prepare, bake and cool cake following package directions for basic recipe. Remove from pan.

3. To assemble, reserve ½ cup each Vanilla and Chocolate frostings; set aside. Place cake on serving plate. Frost half the cake horizontally with remaining Vanilla frosting. Frost remaining half with Chocolate frosting. Place reserved Vanilla frosting in small resealable plastic bag. Repeat with reserved Chocolate frosting. Seal each bag. Knead for 10 seconds. Cut pinpoint hole in bottom corner of each bag. Pipe Chocolate frosting in 10 straight lines to form keys (see Photo). Cut each milk chocolate candy bar into 12 sections by following division marks on bars. Cut 4 sections in half. Place 1 whole and 1 half candy bar section on top of chocolate lines to form black keys as shown. Press vanilla milk chips with points down into Chocolate frosting. Pipe Vanilla frosting above chips to form notes.

> **Tip:** *Use tip of knife to draw straight lines in Vanilla frosting as guide for piping Chocolate frosting.*

Strawberry Meringue Cakes

12 to 16 Servings

1 package Duncan Hines®
   Moist Deluxe Yellow
   Cake Mix
4 eggs, separated
1⅓ cups orange juice
¼ teaspoon cream of tartar

1¼ cups sugar, divided
1 quart fresh strawberries,
   divided
2 cups whipping cream,
   chilled
Mint leaves, for garnish

1. Preheat oven to 350°F. Cut two 14-inch circles of heavy duty aluminum foil; line two 9-inch round cake pans. Grease bottoms and sides of foil; leave 1-inch overhang to form handles.

2. Combine cake mix, egg yolks and orange juice in large bowl. Beat at medium speed with electric mixer for 4 minutes. Pour into pans.

3. Place egg whites and cream of tartar in large bowl. Beat at high speed with electric mixer until soft peaks form. Add 1 cup sugar gradually; beat until stiff peaks form. Spread meringue gently over batter. Bake at 350°F for 35 to 40 minutes or until meringue is golden brown. Cool completely.

4. To assemble, lift edges of aluminum foil to remove cake layers from pans. Carefully remove foil, keeping meringue-side up. Place cakes on serving plates. Reserve several strawberries for garnish. Slice remaining strawberries. Combine whipping cream and remaining ¼ cup sugar in large bowl. Beat at high speed with electric mixer until stiff peaks form. Spread whipped cream mixture on meringue. Arrange strawberry slices in circular pattern on top. Garnish with mint leaves and reserved strawberries. Refrigerate until ready to serve.

> **Tip:** *For ease in lining cake pan, shape aluminum foil to fit by forming over bottom and sides of pan. Remove and place inside pan.*

Strawberry Meringue Cake

Fluffy Black Bottom Pies

16 Servings

1 package Duncan Hines®
    Fudge Brownie Mix,
    Family Size

FILLING

5½ cups (10½ ounce bag)
    miniature marshmallows
1 cup milk
¼ teaspoon salt
2 cups whipping cream,
    chilled

1½ teaspoons vanilla extract
3 squares (1 ounce each)
    semi-sweet chocolate,
    coarsely chopped

TOPPING

1 tablespoon unsweetened
    cocoa, sifted
1 container (8 ounces)
    frozen whipped topping,
    thawed

Semi-sweet chocolate
    shavings, for garnish
Maraschino cherries, well
    drained, for garnish

1. Preheat oven to 350°F. Grease bottoms of two 9-inch pie pans.

2. Prepare brownies following package directions for basic recipe. Spread half the batter evenly in each pie pan. Bake at 350°F for 17 minutes or until set. Cool completely.

3. **For filling,** combine marshmallows, milk and salt in medium saucepan. Cook on low heat, stirring constantly, until marshmallows are melted. Pour mixture into large bowl. Chill until set. Beat whipping cream and vanilla extract in large bowl until stiff peaks form. Fold whipped cream and chopped chocolate into marshmallow mixture. Pour half the mixture evenly over each brownie. Refrigerate at least 4 hours or until set.

4. **For topping,** fold cocoa into whipped topping until blended. Garnish pies with whipped topping mixture, chocolate shavings and maraschino cherries. Refrigerate until ready to serve.

> **Tip:** *For large chocolate shavings, use a vegetable peeler; for fine chocolate shavings, use a hand grater.*

Summer Elegance

1 package Duncan Hines®
  Angel Food Cake Mix
3 cups whipping cream,
  chilled
½ cup *plus* 2 tablespoons
  confectioners sugar
2 teaspoons vanilla extract
2 to 3 drops red food
  coloring

½ cup fresh strawberries,
  mashed
1½ cups quartered, fresh
  strawberries
1 cup fresh raspberries
  Additional fresh
  raspberries, for garnish
  Mint leaves, for garnish

1. Preheat oven to 375°F.

2. Prepare, bake and cool cake following package directions.

3. Place cake on serving plate. Slice 1-inch layer from top of cake; set aside. Cut around cake 1-inch from outer edge, down to 1-inch from bottom. Then, cut around cake 1-inch from inner edge, down to 1-inch from bottom. Lift out cake between cuts with fork leaving 1-inch layer on bottom (see Tip).

4. Combine whipping cream, confectioners sugar, vanilla extract and red food coloring in large bowl. Beat at medium speed with electric mixer until slightly thickened. Add mashed strawberries. Increase speed gradually. Beat until mixture is thick and holds its shape.

5. To assemble, fold quartered strawberries and 1 cup raspberries into 2 cups whipped cream mixture. Fill tunnel of cake. Replace top of cake. Frost sides and top with remaining whipped cream mixture. Refrigerate at least 2 hours. Garnish with additional fresh raspberries and mint leaves just before serving.

Tip: *Place leftover torn cake pieces in resealable plastic bag and freeze. For a quick dessert, serve thawed cake pieces with lightly sugared strawberries.*

Fudgy Pistachio Cake

12 to 16 Servings

CAKE

1 package Duncan Hines® Moist Deluxe White Cake Mix

1 package (4-serving size) pistachio instant pudding and pie filling mix

4 eggs

1 cup water

⅓ cup Crisco® Oil or Crisco® Puritan® Oil

1 can (16 ounces) chocolate syrup

Confectioners sugar, for garnish

FUDGE SAUCE

1 can (12 ounces) evaporated milk

1¾ cups granulated sugar

4 squares (1 ounce each) unsweetened chocolate

¼ cup butter or margarine

1½ teaspoons vanilla extract

¼ teaspoon salt

Chopped pistachio nuts, for garnish

1. Preheat oven to 350°F. Grease and flour 10-inch Bundt® pan.

2. **For cake,** combine cake mix, pudding mix, eggs, water and oil in large bowl. Beat at medium speed with electric mixer for 2 minutes. Pour half the batter into pan. Combine remaining batter and chocolate syrup until blended. Pour over batter in pan. Bake at 350°F for 65 to 70 minutes or until toothpick inserted in center comes out clean. Cool in pan 25 minutes. Invert onto serving plate. Cool completely. Dust with confectioners sugar.

3. **For fudge sauce,** combine evaporated milk and granulated sugar in medium saucepan. Stir constantly on medium heat until mixture comes to a rolling boil. Boil and stir for 1 minute. Add unsweetened chocolate; stir until melted. Beat until smooth. Remove from heat. Stir in butter, vanilla extract and salt.

4. To serve, pour several tablespoons warm fudge sauce on each serving plate. Place cake slices on fudge sauce. Garnish with chopped pistachio nuts. Dust with confectioners sugar.

> **Tip:** *To keep pistachio nuts fresh, store in the freezer.*

Easter Basket Cake

12 to 16 Servings

1 package Duncan Hines®
   Moist Deluxe Cake Mix
   (any flavor)
1 container (16 ounces)
   Duncan Hines® Creamy
   Homestyle Chocolate
   Frosting

Green food coloring
½ teaspoon water
1 cup flaked coconut
   Assorted Easter candies
2 (12-inch) chenille stems
   Pastel ribbon

1. Preheat oven to 350°F. Grease and flour two 9-inch round cake pans.

2. Prepare, bake and cool cake following package directions for basic recipe.

3. Place one cake layer on serving plate. Spread with Chocolate frosting. Top with second cake layer. Frost top with thin layer of frosting. Frost sides and outer 1-inch of cake top with remaining frosting. Make basketweave pattern in frosting with fork tines (see Photo).

4. Combine several drops green food coloring and water in small bowl. Add coconut. Toss with fork until evenly tinted. Place tinted coconut on top of basket for grass. Arrange candies on top.

5. Make handle with chenille stem ends twisted together. Wrap handle with ribbon. Insert in cake. Tie bow on side of handle.

> **Tip:** *To stiffen ribbon for a pretty bow, place ribbon between sheets of waxed paper. With iron set on low heat, press for several seconds.*

Easter Basket Cake

PICNIC SWEETS

❖

Everyone's Favorite Cake   12 to 16 Servings

1 package Duncan Hines®
   Moist Deluxe Yellow
   Cake Mix
1 package (4-serving size)
   vanilla instant pudding
   and pie filling mix
4 eggs
1 cup dairy sour cream
½ cup Crisco® Oil or
   Crisco® Puritan® Oil

2 teaspoons vanilla extract
2 containers (16 ounces
   each) Duncan Hines®
   Creamy Homestyle
   Chocolate Frosting
1 chocolate-covered nougat,
   caramel, peanut candy
   bar, sliced, for garnish

1. Preheat oven to 350°F. Grease and flour two 9-inch square pans.

2. Combine cake mix, pudding mix, eggs, sour cream, oil and vanilla extract in large bowl. Beat at medium speed with electric mixer for 2 minutes. Pour into pans. Bake at 350°F for 33 to 38 minutes or until toothpick inserted in center comes out clean. Cool in pans 15 minutes. Invert onto cooling racks. Cool completely. Place cakes on serving plates.

3. Frost sides and top of each cake with Chocolate frosting. Swirl frosting in diagonal pattern on top. Pull tip of knife through frosting 5 to 7 times to form fan shape. Garnish each cake with slices of candy bar.

> **Tip:** *Store leftover frosting tightly covered in refrigerator. Spread frosting between graham crackers for a quick snack.*

Everyone's Favorite Cake

Creamy Nectarine Torte

12 to 16 Servings

1 package Duncan Hines® Moist Deluxe Yellow Cake Mix
½ cup sugar
¼ cup cornstarch
½ teaspoon ground cinnamon
½ cup water
3¾ cups fresh peeled and chopped nectarines (about 6 to 8 medium)
¼ teaspoon almond extract

1 cup dairy sour cream, divided
¾ cup sliced toasted almonds, divided (see Tip)
1 container (16 ounces) Duncan Hines® Creamy Homestyle Cream Cheese Frosting
Nectarine slices, for garnish

1. Preheat oven to 350°F. Grease and flour two 8-inch round cake pans.

2. Prepare, bake and cool cake following package directions for basic recipe.

3. Combine sugar, cornstarch and cinnamon in large saucepan. Stir in water. Add chopped nectarines. Cook on medium heat, stirring constantly, until clear and thickened. Stir in almond extract. Cool completely.

4. Split each cake layer in half horizontally. Place one cake layer on serving plate. Spread one-third nectarine filling (about 1 cup) to within ½ inch of cake edge. Spread ⅓ cup sour cream over filling. Sprinkle 2 tablespoons almonds over sour cream. Repeat layering 2 more times. Top with remaining cake layer. Frost sides and top with Cream Cheese frosting. Press remaining almonds into frosting on sides of cake. Refrigerate several hours. Garnish with nectarine slices before serving.

Tip: *Toast almonds in 350°F oven on baking sheet for 5 to 7 minutes or until fragrant and light golden brown.*

Creamy Nectarine Torte

Peanut Butter Spritz Sandwiches

1 **package Duncan Hines®**
   Peanut Butter
   Cookie Mix

1 **egg**
3 **bars (1.55 ounces each)**
   milk chocolate

1. Preheat oven to 375°F.

2. Combine cookie mix, contents of peanut butter packet from Mix and egg in large bowl. Stir until thoroughly blended. Fill cookie press with dough. Press desired shapes 2 inches apart onto ungreased baking sheets. Bake at 375°F for 7 to 9 minutes or until set, but not browned. Cool 1 minute on baking sheets.

3. Cut each milk chocolate bar into 12 sections by following division marks on bars.

4. To assemble, carefully remove one cookie from baking sheet. Place one milk chocolate section on bottom of warm cookie; top with second cookie. Press together to make sandwich. Repeat with remaining cookies. Place sandwich cookies on cooling rack until chocolate is set. Store in airtight container.

> **Tip:** *For best appearance, use cookie press plates*
> *that give solid shapes.*

Peanut Butter Spritz Sandwiches

Orange Coconut Cake

1 package Duncan Hines®
   Moist Deluxe Orange
   Supreme Cake Mix
2 eggs
¾ cup water
½ cup orange juice

⅓ cup Crisco® Oil or
   Crisco® Puritan® Oil
1 cup finely chopped pecans
1 cup flaked coconut,
   divided
1 jar (12 ounces) orange
   marmalade, warmed

1. Preheat oven to 350°F. Grease and flour 13×9×2-inch pan.

2. Combine cake mix, eggs, water, orange juice and oil in large bowl. Beat at medium speed with electric mixer for 2 minutes. Stir in pecans and ½ cup coconut. Pour into pan. Bake at 350°F for 35 to 40 minutes or until toothpick inserted in center comes out clean. Cool completely.

3. To serve, cut cake into squares. Spoon warmed marmalade over cake. Sprinkle servings with remaining ½ cup coconut.

Tip: *The flavor of this tender cake is even better the second day.*

Outrageous Angel Food Cake

12 to 16 Servings

CAKE
   1 package Duncan Hines®
      Angel Food Cake Mix

1 envelope unsweetened
   drink mix (any flavor),
   divided (see Tip)

GLAZE
   1 cup confectioners sugar

1 to 2 tablespoons milk

1. Preheat oven to 375°F.

2. **For cake,** combine Cake Flour Mixture (red "B" packet) from Mix and ½ teaspoon dry drink mix in large bowl. Prepare, bake and cool cake following package directions.

3. **For glaze,** combine confectioners sugar and remaining dry drink mix in small bowl. Add milk, 1 teaspoon at a time, stirring until smooth and desired consistency. Drizzle over cake.

Tip: *Let your children choose their favorite color and flavor.*

Orange Coconut Cake

Chocolate Confection Cake   20 to 24 Servings

1 package Duncan Hines®
Moist Deluxe Devil's
Food Cake Mix

FILLING

1 cup evaporated milk
1 cup granulated sugar
24 large marshmallows

1 package (14 ounces)
flaked coconut

TOPPING

½ cup butter or margarine
¼ cup *plus* 2 tablespoons
milk
⅓ cup unsweetened cocoa

1 pound confectioners sugar
(3½ to 4 cups)
1 teaspoon vanilla extract
¾ cup sliced almonds

1. Preheat oven to 350°F. Grease and flour 15½×10½×1-inch jelly-roll pan.

2. Prepare cake following package directions for basic recipe. Pour into pan. Bake at 350°F for 20 to 25 minutes or until toothpick inserted in center comes out clean.

3. **For filling,** combine evaporated milk and granulated sugar in large saucepan. Bring mixture to a boil. Add marshmallows and stir until melted. Stir in coconut. Spread on warm cake.

4. **For topping,** combine butter, milk and cocoa in medium saucepan. Stir on low heat until butter is melted. Add confectioners sugar and vanilla extract, stirring until smooth. Stir in almonds (see Tip). Pour over filling. Spread evenly to edges. Cool completely.

> **Tip:** *For a pretty presentation, sprinkle the ¾ cup almond slices over topping instead of stirring almonds into topping.*

CHILDREN'S *Party* DELIGHTS

✄

Banana Split Cake

12 to 16 Servings

1 package Duncan Hines® Moist Deluxe Banana Supreme Cake Mix
3 eggs
1⅓ cups water
½ cup all-purpose flour
⅓ cup Crisco® Oil or Crisco® Puritan® Oil
1 cup semi-sweet mini chocolate chips

2 to 3 bananas
1 can (16 ounces) chocolate syrup
1 container (8 ounces) frozen whipped topping, thawed
½ cup chopped walnuts
Colored sprinkles
Maraschino cherries with stems, for garnish

1. Preheat oven to 350°F. Grease and flour 13×9×2-inch pan.

2. Combine cake mix, eggs, water, flour and oil in large bowl. Beat at medium speed with electric mixer for 2 minutes. Stir in chocolate chips. Pour into pan. Bake at 350°F for 32 to 35 minutes or until toothpick inserted in center comes out clean. Cool completely.

3. Slice bananas. Cut cake into squares; top with banana slices. Drizzle with chocolate syrup. Top with whipped topping, walnuts and sprinkles. Garnish with maraschino cherries.

Tip: *Dip bananas in diluted lemon juice to prevent darkening.*

Banana Split Cake

Butterfly Cakes

1 package Duncan Hines® Moist Deluxe Cake Mix (any flavor)
1 container (16 ounces) Duncan Hines® Creamy Homestyle Vanilla Frosting, divided
Assorted candies such as chocolate chips, peanut butter chips, vanilla milk chips, halved gumdrops, halved jelly beans and candy-coated chocolate pieces
4 bars (2 to 2½ ounces each) chocolate-covered crunchy peanut butter candy
4 chocolate-covered peanut butter cups
Spaghetti (uncooked)

1. Preheat oven to 350°F. Grease and flour two 9-inch round cake pans.

2. Prepare, bake and cool cake following package directions for basic recipe.

3. To assemble, cut each cake in half to form 2 semicircles (see Tip). Arrange on serving platters (see Photo). Reserve 1 tablespoon Vanilla frosting for candies. Frost sides and tops of cakes with remaining frosting. Use tip of knife to mark sections of wings. Decorate each section with candy pieces. Spread reserved frosting on flat side of one candy bar. Top with second candy bar; press together. Repeat with remaining candy bars. Place between cake semicircles for bodies. Spread reserved frosting on flat side of one peanut butter cup. Top with second peanut butter cup; press together. Repeat with remaining peanut butter cups. Place at top end of candy bars for heads. Use vanilla milk chips for eyes and spaghetti for antennas.

> **Tip:** *Cakes are easier to frost when completely frozen. After cutting into semicircles, return to freezer while organizing candies for decorations.*

Butterfly Cake

"Go Fly a Kite" Cake

12 to 16 Servings

1 package Duncan Hines®
  Moist Deluxe Cake Mix
  (any flavor)
2 containers (16 ounces
  each) Duncan Hines®
  Creamy Homestyle
  Vanilla Frosting, divided

Blue and yellow food
  coloring (see Tip)
Pretzel sticks
Red licorice lace
Assorted colored decors

1. Preheat oven to 350°F. Grease and flour 15½×10½×1-inch jelly-roll pan.

2. Prepare cake following package directions for basic recipe. Pour into pan. Bake at 350°F for 18 to 22 minutes or until toothpick inserted in center comes out clean. Cool in pan 15 minutes. Invert onto cooling rack. Cool completely.

3. Tint 1⅓ cups Vanilla frosting with blue food coloring; set aside. Tint remaining Vanilla frosting with yellow food coloring.

4. Measure shorter sides of cake rectangle to determine centers and mark with toothpicks. Cut cake from marked centers to opposite sides creating four triangles (see Diagram 1). Place kite-shaped layer on large serving tray. Spread top with yellow frosting.

5. To assemble second layer, arrange triangles on cake (see Diagram 2). Frost sides and tops of areas 1 and 3 with yellow frosting. Repeat for areas 2 and 4 with blue frosting. Place pretzel sticks in cross shape to form wood frame. Place red licorice lace to form kite tail. Decorate with assorted colored decors.

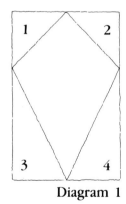

Diagram 1

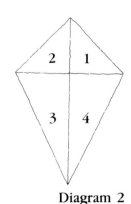

Diagram 2

Tip: *To control the color of tinted frostings, use only 1 to 2 drops of food coloring at a time. Stir frosting until color is thoroughly blended before adding more drops.*

Surprise-Filled Cupcakes

24 Cupcakes

1 package Duncan Hines®
    Moist Deluxe Dark
    Dutch Fudge Cake Mix
1 jar (7 ounces)
    marshmallow creme,
    divided

1 container (16 ounces)
    Duncan Hines® Creamy
    Homestyle Dark
    Chocolate Frosting
½ cup confectioners sugar
2½ teaspoons milk

1. Preheat oven to 350°F. Place 24 (2½-inch) paper liners in muffin cups.

2. Prepare, bake and cool cupcakes following package directions for basic recipe.

3. Reserve 2 tablespoons marshmallow creme; set aside. Place remaining marshmallow creme in decorating bag fitted with large star tip. Push tip in top center of each cupcake about 1-inch deep. Tightly squeeze bag for 5 to 7 seconds to fill cupcake.

4. Frost cupcakes with Dark Chocolate frosting. Combine reserved marshmallow creme and confectioners sugar in small bowl. Add milk, 1 teaspoon at a time, stirring until smooth. Place in small resealable plastic bag. Snip pinpoint hole in corner of bag. Squeeze design over each cupcake.

> **Tip:** *For an extra surprise, tint marshmallow creme filling with a few drops of your favorite food coloring.*

Lemon Sunshine Cake

12 to 16 Servings

1 package Duncan Hines®
    Moist Deluxe Lemon
    Supreme Cake Mix
5 cups confectioners sugar
¾ cup Crisco® Shortening
⅓ cup non-dairy powdered
    creamer
¼ cup lemon juice
¼ cup *plus* ¾ teaspoon
    water, divided

½ teaspoon salt
    Yellow food coloring
1½ cups flaked coconut
2 mandarin orange
    segments
2 small blue candies
1 maraschino cherry,
    drained
½ orange slice
    Red licorice lace

1. Preheat oven to 350°F. Grease and flour two 8-inch round cake pans.

2. Prepare, bake and cool cake following package directions for basic recipe. Freeze one layer.

3. For frosting, combine confectioners sugar, shortening, non-dairy powdered creamer, lemon juice, ¼ cup water and salt in large bowl. Beat at medium speed with electric mixer for 3 minutes. Beat at high speed for 5 minutes. Add more confectioners sugar to thicken or more water to thin, as needed. Tint frosting with yellow food coloring to desired color. To tint coconut, combine several drops yellow food coloring and remaining ¾ teaspoon water in small bowl. Add coconut. Toss with fork.

4. To assemble, place unfrozen cake layer in center of 16-inch round serving plate. Frost sides and top with 1 cup frosting. Cut frozen cake layer into 8 equal wedges (see Diagram). Trim curved side of each wedge to fit round layer. Place wedges around cake to form sun as shown. Frost cake wedges. Press coconut on sides of wedges. Arrange mandarin oranges and small blue candies for eyes, cherry for nose, orange slice for mouth and licorice for eyebrows.

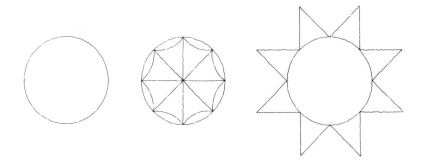

Tip: *For variety, choose your own assortment of candy.*

Lemon Sunshine Cake

Domino Brownie Cake

24 to 32 Servings

1 package Duncan Hines®
    Fudge Brownie Mix,
    Family Size
1 package Duncan Hines®
    Moist Deluxe Butter
    Recipe Fudge Cake Mix
1 container (16 ounces)
    Duncan Hines® Creamy
    Homestyle Dark
    Chocolate Frosting

1 container (16 ounces)
    Duncan Hines® Creamy
    Homestyle Cream
    Cheese Frosting, divided
Vanilla milk chips

1. Preheat oven to 350°F. Grease 13×9×2-inch pan.

2. Prepare, bake and cool brownies following package directions for basic recipe.

3. Preheat oven to 375°F. Grease and flour 13×9×2-inch pan.

4. Prepare, bake and cool cake following package directions for basic recipe. Remove from pan.

5. Spread Dark Chocolate frosting on brownies. Refrigerate until frosting is firm. Cut into 32 bars. Remove from pan. Place ½ cup Cream Cheese frosting in small resealable plastic bag. Knead frosting in bag for 10 seconds. Snip pinpoint hole in corner of bag. Pipe frosting to make center line on each brownie for domino (see Photo). Press vanilla milk chips with points down into fudge frosting for dots.

6. To assemble, frost sides and top of cake with remaining Cream Cheese frosting. Arrange domino brownies on top of and around cake, as desired.

Tip: *For ease in cutting brownies, make sure they are well chilled and use a knife with a thin, sharp blade.*

❉

CHILDREN'S PARTY DELIGHTS 87

Peanut Butter Pizza Cookies

18 (3-Inch) Cookies

2 packages Duncan Hines® Peanut Butter Cookie Mix
2 eggs
1 tablespoon water
   Sugar
1 container (16 ounces) Duncan Hines® Creamy Homestyle Chocolate Frosting

Cashews
Candy-coated chocolate pieces
Gumdrops, halved
Flaked coconut
1 bar (2 ounces) white chocolate baking bar
1 tablespoon Crisco® Shortening

1. Preheat oven to 375°F.

2. For cookies, place cookie mixes in large bowl. Break up any lumps. Add eggs, contents of peanut butter packets from Mixes and water. Stir until thoroughly blended. Shape into 18 (2-inch) balls (about 3 level tablespoons each). Place 3½ inches apart on ungreased baking sheets. Flatten with bottom of large glass dipped in sugar to make 3-inch circles. Bake at 375°F for 9 to 11 minutes or until set. Cool 1 minute on baking sheets. Remove to cooling racks. Cool completely.

3. Frost cookies with Chocolate frosting. Decorate with cashews, candy pieces, gumdrops and coconut. Melt white chocolate and shortening in small saucepan on low heat, stirring constantly, until smooth. Drizzle over cookies. Store between layers of waxed paper in airtight container.

> **Tip:** *To melt white chocolate in microwave, place in microwave-safe bowl. Add shortening. Microwave at DEFROST (30% power) for 5 minutes. Stir well. Microwave at DEFROST (30% power) for 1 to 2 minutes longer, stirring every minute until smooth.*

Turtle Cake

1 package Duncan Hines®
Moist Deluxe Fudge
Marble Cake Mix
6 fun size chocolate-covered
nougat, caramel, peanut
candy bars
1 container (16 ounces)
Duncan Hines® Creamy
Homestyle Cream
Cheese Frosting, divided

Green food coloring
2 tablespoons slivered
almonds
Candy-coated chocolate
pieces
Vanilla milk chips

1. Preheat oven to 350°F. Grease and flour 2½-quart ovenproof glass bowl with rounded bottom.

2. Prepare cake following package directions for basic recipe. Pour into bowl. Bake at 350°F for 55 to 60 minutes or until toothpick inserted in center comes out clean. Cool in bowl 20 minutes. Invert onto cooling rack. Cool completely.

3. To assemble, place cake on serving plate. Remove 1-inch cake square from upper side of cake for head. Insert 2 fun size candy bars, flat sides together, into square hole for head. Position remaining 4 candy bars under cake for feet. Reserve 1 teaspoon Cream Cheese frosting. Tint remaining Cream Cheese frosting with green food coloring; frost cake. Sprinkle almonds on top. Place candy-coated chocolate pieces around bottom edge of shell. Attach vanilla milk chips to head with reserved frosting for eyes.

Tip: *For a brighter green frosting, use green paste food color available from cake decorating and specialty shops.*

Chocolate Cream-Filled Squares

24 Servings

**1 package Duncan Hines®
Moist Deluxe Devil's
Food Cake Mix**

FILLING

½ cup butter or margarine,
softened
½ cup Crisco® Shortening
1 cup granulated sugar

2 cans (5 ounces each)
evaporated milk
(1¼ cups)
1 tablespoon vanilla extract

GLAZE

2 cups sifted confectioners
sugar
2 packets (1 ounce each)
unsweetened pre-melted
chocolate

¼ cup hot melted butter
¼ cup boiling water, divided

1. Preheat oven to 350°F. Grease and flour 15½×10½×1-inch jelly-roll pan.

2. Prepare cake following package directions for basic recipe. Pour batter into pan. Bake at 350°F for 20 to 24 minutes or until toothpick inserted in center comes out clean. Cool completely.

3. **For filling,** place ½ cup butter in large bowl. Beat at medium speed with electric mixer for 5 minutes. Add shortening gradually, beating for 4 minutes. Add granulated sugar gradually, beating until well blended. Add evaporated milk and vanilla extract. (It is normal for mixture to separate.) Beat for 8 minutes or until smooth and creamy. Spread over cake. Refrigerate.

4. **For glaze,** combine confectioners sugar, pre-melted chocolate, melted butter and 3 tablespoons boiling water in small bowl. Stir until blended. Add remaining 1 tablespoon water. Beat until smooth. Spread immediately over filling. Refrigerate until ready to serve.

> **Tip:** *You may also bake this cake in a greased and floured 13×9×2-inch pan at 350°F for 35 to 38 minutes or until toothpick inserted in center comes out clean.*

A "Beary" Special Cake

12 to 16 Servings

1 package Duncan Hines®
  Moist Deluxe Cake Mix
  (any flavor)
1 container (16 ounces)
  Duncan Hines® Creamy
  Homestyle Frosting
  (any flavor)

Assorted gumdrops,
  halved
Teddy-shaped graham
  snacks (see Tip)

1. Preheat oven to 350°F. Grease and flour two 9-inch round cake pans.

2. Prepare, bake and cool cake following package directions for basic recipe.

3. To assemble, place one cake layer on serving plate. Spread with one-third of frosting. Top with second cake layer. Frost sides and top with remaining frosting. Decorate with alternating rows of gumdrops and teddy-shaped graham snacks.

> **Tip:** *To add interest, use chocolate-flavored graham snacks with Duncan Hines® Vanilla frosting, or vanilla-flavored graham snacks with Duncan Hines® Chocolate frosting.*

Chocolate Chip Pretzel Cookies

36 Cookies

1 package Duncan Hines®
  Chocolate Chip
  Cookie Mix
1 egg

2 teaspoons water
¾ cup coarsely broken thin
  pretzel sticks (see Tip)

1. Preheat oven to 375°F.

2. Combine cookie mix, contents of buttery flavor packet from Mix, egg and water in large bowl. Stir until thoroughly blended. Stir in pretzels. Drop by rounded teaspoonfuls 2 inches apart onto ungreased baking sheets. Bake at 375°F for 8 to 10 minutes or until light golden brown. Cool 1 minute on baking sheets. Remove to cooling racks. Cool completely. Store in airtight container.

> **Tip:** *Place pretzels in a resealable plastic bag; crush with a rolling pin.*

RECIPE INDEX

DUNCAN HINES INDEX